THE RETURN OF THE NAKED MAN

THE RETURN OF THE NAKED MAN

Robert Tremmel

BRICK ROAD
POETRY PRESS

Brick Road Poetry Press
www.brickroadpoetrypress.com

Cover art: "Railway Track with the moon and milky way in night sky"
©nuttawutnuy - stock.adobe.com

Author photo: © Nick Tremmel

Library of Congress Control Number: 2021934513
ISBN: 978-1-950739-04-2

Published by Brick Road Poetry Press
341 Lee Road 553
Phenix City, AL 36867
www.brickroadpoetrypress.com

Brick Road logo by Dwight New

For Michelle
Many more happy returns!

Table of Contents

Part 1: The End

Part 2: The Beginning

Part 3: The Naked Man Gets Religion

Part 4: The End

Even if you are pure and naked, bare and clean, without mental activity outside of things, without things outside of mental activity, you still have not escaped standing by a stump waiting for a rabbit.

The Blue Cliff Record, Case 95

Part 1

The End

Escape

There is a naked man
loaded and locked
in his casket
like an astronaut
wheeling unassisted
up the center aisle
toward the front door
of St. Patrick's church.

In the pews
the people stand amazed
as usual, some
cry, others daydream
about the ham
sandwiches stacked
in the parish hall
and so, the organist sinks
her long, muscular fingers
into the keyboard
and grinds out *Amazing Grace*
for the third time in a week.

The priest stays close
to the holy water
just in case
but the naked man
has gathered his mind
and has no intention
of further disrupting
the teachings of the Church.

He has finally
gotten away and intends
to stay away.

His tie is loose, his eyes
closed, lips sewed shut
in a tight smile.

His hands
are perfectly still
for the very first time
and crossed upon his chest.

Alternate Ending

There is a naked man
inside a one-size-fits-all
cardboard coffin, sliding
into the crematorium
and humming
On Eagle's Wings
with the rush of gas.

He is cool as air, hot
as fire, fast
as smoke, light as ash.

Part 2

The Beginning

The naked man is back

from his contractual
obligations, long
casket rides up the aisle

into the fire

and then on
over the rooftops
to the edge of town
and then on once more
to the edge of doom
and doom's heartland
where the earth cracks open
and more fire bubbles

the breath catches
and sizzles

the flesh burns

and there is a stench
that will wake
even the dead

especially the dead.

Early 21st Century

There is a naked man
sitting in his pick-up
parked on a promontory
overlooking the ocean.

He has been there
a long time, facing
west, or maybe east
with the engine running
and his foot on the gas.

From time to time, for reasons
known only to him
or not, he presses
the accelerator
all the way
to the firewall
and holds it there, making
the engine scream
at majorpsychosisthreshold.

Then, maybe for days
he backs off
and just lets it idle
as clouds blow over him
and the sun either rises
or sets and the air
around him boils with exhaust.

Saturday Night

There is a naked man
out in his garden
with an open bottle
of Budweiser
and an old pie pan
from Baker's Square.

As the sun begins
to tilt toward evening
the naked man
tilts the bottle
over the pie pan
like a priest
over the chalice
and pours out half.

Then he stands, drains
the other half and thinks
about his drinking buddies
the slugs, already
stirring deep beneath
the lettuce leaves, aroused
by the scent of beer
and starting to make plans
for the short trip up
to the darkening air
and a long, slow night
of carousing, orgy
and drowning.

The Good Old Days

There is a naked man
sitting through a meeting
where a woman
he can't stand
is saying something
he disagrees with
to a man
he can't stand either.

So, the naked man
reads the posters
on the wall

studies the cheap
reproductions
of mediocre paintings

and fantasizes
about a meeting
years ago, when someone
set out a plate of cookies
the naked man didn't like
and refused to eat.

Bottom Line

There is a naked man
sitting through yet
another meeting.

The topic
as usual
is the budget.

Once again, the bottom line
is that there is
no bottom line.

More cuts must be made
but into muscle
and bone this time.

All the fat
was sliced away
long ago.

The naked man
looks over
at the naked
woman's hands
beside him and notes
the lean, sculpted
fingers, so well-endowed
with muscle and bone
he can barely
keep himself
from reaching out
and touching them
just to see

what they feel like
before they are gone.

Bowls

There is a naked man
making breakfast
in his kitchen, again

measuring cereal
and spooning fruit
into bowls the color
of his own skin.

It has been three days
since the naked man's soul
was sucked out of his body
by an all-day meeting
and replaced with an organ
that whistles when he breathes
and eats his flesh
from the inside.

Still, like the woman's hands
he can't help but notice
how brightly the raspberries
he picked last evening shine

and how happy
they seem, even though
they too are being consumed.

Somewhere There Is This Lake

There is a naked man
sitting through yet another
meeting, and this time
the boss is running
a few numbers.

Power flows from her power
point slides, bar graphs, pie
charts, red numbers, black
numbers, green numbers

blank numbers

these numbers are up
but don't add up

these numbers are down
and broken down

data points, decimal
points like bullet holes

and at some point
the naked man
realizes the boss's
numbers don't add up
and her mind
is completely riddled
with bullet points
and she is pointedly
ignorant of the riddle
and infinite points
that are the naked man

himself, sitting there
in a straight-backed
chair, silently
watching the drama
and the riddle
of the infinite points
that are the woman
sitting in front of him

the contours
of her auburn hair
streaked with gold currents
all flowing downhill
into a cold quiet lake
resting in the shade
of tall trees, the rush
of wind over
the water and the flash
of a secretive
ouzel's quick grey wings.

New Year's Day

1982

There is a naked man
standing in *Arroyo Seco*
with zoom binoculars.

He is amazed
at the coolliquidsilk
feel of low clouds
flowing through sunlight.

Off to his left
men in tuxedos
and women in gowns
sit down at a table
set up on the grass
and decked out
with silver and crystal.

A waiter pours
sparkling wine, cradling
the neck of the bottle
on a thick, white towel.

To the naked man's right
a white limousine
with eight motorcycle
police pulls up
and Jimmy Stewart, dressed
in white trousers and a white
coat with tails, steps out
under the liquid sky just
as the San Gabriels

melt into it like buffalo
entering the prairie.

January 2

Twenty Years Later

There is a naked man
standing in a crowd
outside yet another
stadium about sunset.

He leans against
barricades set up across
from the satellite trucks.

The sports anchor
from Channel 8
back home steps out
under a nylon
canopy and waves

and the naked man
waves back at her with a big
smile and the proper
enthusiasm.

Suddenly, police
on motorcycles
in a column of twos
come pouring down the chute
between the trucks
and the barricades

at least twenty pairs
interspersed with cruisers
and SUVs, all dark
tinted glass and bristling

with antennas.

Finally, the buses
start rolling in
and the naked man
knows nothing else
but to cry out
until his throat hurts
and his life that day is done
passing before his eyes.

Near-Death Experience

There is a naked man
leaving the stadium
down-in-the-mouth
and at the corners
of his eyes.

Once again
the naked man's team
was dragged lifeless
from the field, one
player at a time.

Down on the tracks
the train is idling.

Swarms of down-in-the-mouthers
drag themselves across
the small concrete
platform to the metal
steps, step up like cattle
in a chute
with one last effort
and disappear.

The naked man crosses
the bridge above them
and enters a tree
that has lost its leaves
and even though he has no

idea where he is
the naked man is not
the first to arrive
and he is not alone.

Tuning into the Past

There is a naked man
out in his shed on a cold
Saturday afternoon
in early March.

He hasn't shaved
his grey beard for two days
and is tired
of the snow still drifted
thigh deep down from the house
and now rain is starting
to fall out of low dark clouds.

The naked man is busy
working on his tractor
under the light
of a single bare
bulb, installing
spark plugs and air cleaner
and bolting on
freshly sharpened blades
wet down with WD-40.

At exactly 2:00 P.M.
the naked man stands
and looks out
the door, which is lower
than he is tall, aims
his CC Radio Plus
at a remote point
three-hundred
miles east, punches in

7:20 AM
and turns the volume up.

Chicago Cubs baseball
is on the air
from HoHoKam Park
in Mesa, Arizona.

Along with Cubs Legend
and Hall-of-Famer
Ron Santo
this is Pat Hughes reporting.

The sky here
is the same color blue
as Lake Michigan
in June, with sail boats
all over and people
eating tuna sandwiches
and your life too
whether you believe it or not
is about to end
and then begin again.

Attention, Attention

There is a naked man
at yet another ballgame.

This time
it is spring
and evening, complete
with warm and cool
breezes blowing
simultaneously
from the west, spotlights
shining on the gold
dome across
the river, high above
the center field fence.

In the sixth inning
the naked man
goes down to the restroom
behind third base
and steps across the wet
sticky floor, just
as a man standing
at a urinal shakes, zips
up, bends over, grabs
his beer from between
his feet and walks away
whistling a tune
that has been stuck
in his mind
for a hundred-thousand years
and maybe more.

April

There is a naked man
sitting through yet
another meeting.

On the wall
is a calendar
and this month
the picture
is a puppy running
on green, spring grass.

Even though
the naked man
tries hard to believe
the puppy is happy
and there are kind people
just beyond the page

maybe in May

and even though he repeats
words to himself
like *frolicking*
and *free* as a mantra
of his most fervent desire

there is something unsettling
about the way
this puppy holds
its head, the set
of its jaw
and the worry

yes, definitely
the deep worry
in the puppy's eyes.

Puppies

There is a naked man
raising puppies
in his backyard.

Some of these puppies
he teaches to hunt
by explaining in great
detail the intricate
interrelationships
of wind and scent, how
a covey rise air-washes
singles and variable
winds turn cover
into a kaleidoscope
of contradictions
and chaos.

And still others
he teaches
to lie quietly all day
and move from window
to window, door to door
as the earth and sun move
and the floor below
goes from cold
to warm, warm
to cold, cold
to warm, warm
to cold.

Appetite

There is a naked man
still hungry
after a breakfast
of oatmeal, poached
eggs and tea.

He is thinking
how good a beer
might taste
right now, and then
some pickled herring

a handful
of peanuts, maybe
three or four smoked almonds
followed by a salad made
with Mediterranean
greens, balsamic
vinaigrette, then rice
and snow peas roasted
in the stomach
of a blind goat.

When he finishes
his tea, the naked man goes
to the closet, pulls out
the coat that always
has a knife in the pocket
and heads down
across the yard
to where the neighbor's fence
angles through cottonwoods

that cast haphazard
shadows on a chaos
of hoofmarks, debris
and random
patches of newly
cleared ground.

Pulp Fiction

For Monique

There is a naked man
eating oatmeal
at the breakfast table.

As he eats he begins
listening to the woman
across from him, who begins
talking about how many
thousand tons of wood chips
she will need this week to keep
her pulp plant running

how many air and oil
filters they will make
with her pulp, how many
toilet seats
and adult diapers
she can get
out of a single tree

but by the time she passes
that point, the naked man
is already miles behind
thinking about shade, how
it might be on a summer
afternoon to stand
beneath a diaper tree

or maybe just
sit down, lean
back against the bark

and feel the even stroke
of a mighty engine
pumping clear and clean
through miles and miles of veins.

The naked man stops to talk

to the black man
fishing the lake.

He has a bucketful
of small, speckled fish
swimming in clear water
and many opinions.

The naked man has opinions
of his own, but doesn't
bring them up
except for one or two

nor does he question
the meal worms the man
is using for bait.

The fish do not question
the meal worms either

and the meal worms
have nothing to say.

The sun shines
on the water, the sand

the fish, the worms
and the black man

the nearly
invisible moon
and also the naked man.

Shore Lunch

There is a naked woman
watching a naked chef
on television.

About half-way through
the broiled walleye
and mushrooms
they both reach
for salt, scales fall
from their naked eyes
and they realize
that to everyone else
they appear clothed
and perfectly normal
and only they can see
the gill slits
that ripple wild
with invisible
current flowing
through shadows cast
by moonlight across
vast and nearly boundless
acres of sand.

Oryoki

There is a naked man
opening his bowls, spreading
the cloth, lifting
the smallest bowl out
and placing it
to the right, the larger
to its left
and cradling the largest
like a baby's head
and setting it gently down
to the far left, gently
gently as the earth
would receive a leaf

three planets in perfect
synchronous orbit.

He wishes this moment
could last forever
with the last bell still
reverberating, clear
sky inside
and outside, hunger
the perfect companion
and the future
shiny as black
enamel, clean
and completely at rest

but always the food arrives
at the door, the chant begins.

Tipping

There is a naked man
driving across
Mohawk-Niagara late
on a summer morning.

Even though this
is his first time through
and he is miles
from the point of contact
he can feel power
unfolding from rock
and rushing water, crouching
mountains, the angle
of sun glancing across
the nose of his truck
and ricocheting deep
into the galaxy.

Off to his right
two buzzards spiral
down a hundred feet
to get a closer look
at something hidden
in the timber.

Now what? the naked man
asks himself
as he pours his life straight
down the road and tips
on the fulcrum
of yet another day.

Crossing the Missouri

There is a naked man
on board an eastbound flight
from San Francisco.

He is going home
after too many days
in bad-air hotels
and sardine-can
slab houses
with broken locks
and underpowered
furnaces belching
cold, cracker dry air.

As he starts to descend
his head swells to the size
of a toilet bowl, his eyes
water and his sinuses
begin a long sermon
about intemperate
behavior, body fluids
and the wages of sin.

Out the window, he sees
row upon row of mighty
fortresses, each one
set deep in solid
ground, each one flying
a flag the color of smoke
and clouds, the shape
of the northwind.

Forecast

There is a naked man
with a pain in his gut.

The doctor
in her white coat looks
at how he sits, slumped
over in his grade-
school-sized chair next
to the blood pressure cuff
and the latex gloves
already out of the box.

Then the poking, the blood
draw, x-ray right away

cup of poison
and CT scan

and sure enough:
it is confirmed.

The naked man
has a pain in his gut

a bad one.

Out in the parking lot
the naked man's truck
heats up in the August
sun, hazy flow
of gulf moisture

spicy food, music
from golden horns

but when it will rain
no one knows.

Buying Gas and Ice at the Kwik & EZ

There is a naked man
standing in line
late at night.

At the cash register
next to him, a heavy
woman has placed
a small child
on the counter.
A second child
rifles through bags
of cookies and chips.

She is howling
because her mother
has selected
cookies and chips not
to her liking.

The child on the counter
is wearing a filthy shirt
and her diaper at best
needs changing.

After he pays
and turns to leave
the naked man
decides to give
the gourmet
in the cookies and chips
plenty of room.

As if she can read
his mind, she howls
louder and louder
until she calls out
the naked man's
very own name

as if he were her father
and she flesh
of his very own flesh.

Out on the Street

There is a naked man
sitting in a booth
next to a window.

Outside, it is already
getting dark.

Tired men wrapped in heavy
coats and wearing newly
sober faces pass by
on the street, smoking
cigarettes and looking
for someone new
to talk to.

One of them parks
his wheel chair right
outside the window
the naked man is inside
sitting next to
and smokes into the wind.

Only inches
separate the naked man
from the smoking man
who has one white
marble in his pocket
and stumps for legs.

A ten-foot tall Buddha
facing the bar raises
his right hand and opens
his left hand on his knee.

Pour this man
a cup of tea, he says

take him a fresh roll
with sweet potato
in the center
and deliver him
from evil.

In the Bedroom

There is a naked woman
in the kitchen, talking
on the phone with the lights out.

How she got there
and exactly why
she remains is not clear.

She has been there a long
time, though, the season
has changed and now it is far
too dark for the naked man
left behind in the bedroom
to hear what she is talking about.

Out in the street
a car drives by
with the volume
turned up so high
the naked man
can pick up a few bars
of lyrics, something
about another naked man
who disappeared one day
as if he had died, wandered
city streets and mountain
trails, followed by hummingbirds
and clouds of mosquitoes

and later on he can still feel
the bass from blocks away
through closed windows

and darkness that will thicken
and grow colder
than he can imagine
and through it all
the naked woman
will talk on
and he will love her for it
without knowing why
or caring that he does not.

High Altitude Bombing

There is a naked man
standing thigh deep
in muddy water, casting
and retrieving, casting
and retrieving, calling
and waiting for even
the weakest response

reading shadows
within the shadows

sorting fish tugs
from twigs, turtle heads
from snake heads, carp
making bright fluorescent Os
with their lips, walleyes
with ancient secrets
when all of a sudden
the surface explodes
around him in a pattern
of hard white drops
that fade into the water
like puffs of smoke
on a windless day
and far above
a flock of buzzards
with a single mind
far deeper
than the naked man
can wade or cast
or reach wheels
away, passes

beyond his sight
and leaves him
neither alive
nor dead
nor anywhere
in between.

Part 3

The Naked Man Gets Religion

Blue Votives

There is a naked man
kneeling in the back
of the church, alone.

He feels the rough tiles
pressing the calluses
on his knees and prays
to the Zen Master
who died with calluses
on his forehead.

There is no response.

How could there be?

The Zen Master never
even heard of prayer
when he was alive
and death, the naked man
is beginning to realize
is not much of a place
for prayer either.

All around the naked man
votives bloom in small
blue vases, gutter down
and go out.

The naked man shoves more
coins through the slot, lights
more candles and goes to find

the stations of the cross
and a place he can rest.

Years later, when he gets there
number nine seems
to hold some promise.

Healing

There is a naked woman
carrying a pecan pie
up the stairs
from the basement.

This is not
her pecan pie.
She did not bake it
and she will not eat it.

She will, in fact
have nothing
to do with it

except carry it
up the stairs
and hand it away
like someone else
might have a tumor
removed, a rotten
tooth, infected
appendix, or a mole.

Passing On

There is a naked man
passing down
the hallway, clenching
his fists, grinding
his teeth, as tears
pour down his cheeks.

He passes rooms
on the right and left

prostitutes groaning
at appropriate times

the hum of monitors
and the gurgling
and dripping of tubes
and ventilators

more groaning

click of tired
fingers on keyboards

mouse click, silent
scrolling of hands
through thinning
hair, sagging
slumping body parts.

The hallway is endless.

The naked man is exhausted.

The soles of his feet burn
with blisters, his ears ring
with the suffering
all around him.

His knees ache, he longs
to kneel down
at the end of each step
but he keeps passing on.

Ruling

There is a naked man
in pain again
and worrying
about his health.

Each day
he begins to worry
at the breakfast table
and then takes his worry
to work, where he gets up
every hour or so
to stand and worry
in the restroom.

Later, he returns home
and takes his worry
like a little child, out
into the backyard
between the garden
and the white swamp oak
he planted last fall
and worried about
all winter, wondering
why it wants
to lean toward the south.

And still later
when the sun has gone down
the naked man sits
in his chair to read
and worry
and finally

is able to worry
that too much worry
all by itself
could kill him
and then, whether or not
a death like that
would be ruled
a suicide
or simply
attributed to natural causes.

Connemara

There is a naked man
praying on the strand
between Omey Island
and the Star of the Sea.

Behind him, Mass drones on
like the tide lapping
at his knees.

Ahead, he can just
barely make out
a fallen cottage
in the fog, ruins
of a fence, scattering
of crosses among stones
and remnants of stones
and gravesites so small
not even a child
could find room enough to rest
except by sinking
far, far below.

Forgiveness

There is a naked man
on his knees in a dark room
built of stone at the edge
of the water, confessing
his sin to God again
and again, God listens
to what the naked man
has to say and forgives him
but the naked man
just keeps praying
and confessing, groaning
each time he relives
his sin, watching it
unfold each time
exactly the same way
and each time
he curses himself
exactly the same way
with exactly the same curse
and then the same guilt rises
in his throat, eats
through his flesh, picks
at his organs
and scatters his bones
and each time
when it is over
the Beautiful Buzzard
of the Dark hoists its body
up from the edge
of the water, climbs
in a wide, slow spiral

over the trees, back
to the dark procession
and then tips back
and forth in a gentle
crosswind, the constantly
changing light
and keeps looking down
where the naked man
is always waiting
on his knees in a dark
room built of stone
at the edge of the water.

Benediction

There is a naked man
walking down a hall
in a large city hospital.

At every open door
the naked man pauses
to look in, utter
a few quiet words
and raise his hand
in his own personal
gestures of benediction.

At some of the doors
the people inside are so
tangled up in tubes and wires
and their own suffering
they ignore the naked man
and do not even look up
when he appears.

At other doors the people
curse the naked man
and tell him to go to hell
or at least dust off his shoes
and move on, which he does
with eager steps, raising
his hand one more time.

And still others smile
when they see the naked man
and accept his blessing
with relief, invite him in

to sit awhile, eat
a fresh cookie, taste
a little glass of sweet
homemade wine that heals
all wounds, warms the hands
and feet and calms the mind.

Footprints in the Sand

There is a naked man
walking along a beach
with Jesus.

The sun seems way
too bright, the sand
too hot, the water
dirty and Jesus
is having a bad day.

After all, he is human too:
his head hurts, his feet
stink, his hands bleed and he
is feeling forsaken
and double-crossed.

Finally, the naked man
gets tired of the limping
and whining, picks Jesus
up and throws him
over his shoulder.

They plod on
in silence to the top
of a small dune
where the naked man turns
to look back and is amazed.

There are two sets
of footprints
in the distance
but from the point
where he began

to carry Jesus
the sand is unbroken, clear
as a blank disk
and deep inside
the naked man realizes
that when the tide rises
it will again write
whatever it wants to write
and will erase
whatever it decides.

Saturday, Bay City

There is a naked man
standing on the far bank
of the Saginaw River.

Behind him, dozens
of kids sledding
on high steep
hills chase
their shadows down
through late afternoon.

In front of him
twenty-seven
ice fishing shelters
all zipped up
against the north wind
are spread out on the river.

Every few minutes
snowmobiles in twos and threes
shoot past him up and down
the river into the falling
light and breathless future
everyone knows is coming.

The naked man looks
at his watch and sees
he has another
thirty-two minutes
before he must leave
and cross the river
to the empty

downtown, the narrow
stairs he must climb
and the lonely room
he must visit
on the other side.

Metamorphosis

There is a naked man
walking down a hallway
who looks into an office
and sees the woman
he always sees there
sitting at her computer
and staring into the face
of a wolf that covers
the whole screen
and the wolf stares back
without blinking and no
expression, just
as it always does
and to the naked man
it seems that each day
the wolf looks just
a little bit more
like the woman
and the woman just
a little bit more
like the wolf
until he begins
to admire the way
the long, grey hairs
give depth to her face
and to wonder what
it will be like
when all their eyes are blue
and sword shaped, with flames

rimming the edges
and pupils of heavy
gravity black.

Toad in the Snow

There is a naked man
sitting at his window
with the blinds pulled up
watching the snow fall
in dry, tight grains
that sift down and fill
each tiny hiding place
and pocket of still air
and as it falls
it is also
covering a toad
crouched beside the garden.

Even though
the naked man
wants very badly
to go outside and see
if the toad is alive
or dead or somewhere
in between
there is something looming
just beyond the range
of his vision
that holds him back
as the toad slowly, so
slowly, disappears.

Part 4

The End and Beyond

Silence

There is a naked man
so sick he stays
inside himself all day
and walks from one white wall
to another, studying
the silence, the flat expanse
of white and the clean
right angles, white trim
and the empty window

long spider legs
of cactus crawling
silently across
the glass-topped table
in light
from the empty window

blooms on the cactus
pulsing like organs, nail
holes in the walls
the caliber
of arteries

the polished floor
and the empty window

the kanji for silence
brushed in black ink
on the white wall

of the empty window

the silence itself
and the silence
within that.

Walking In Complete Darkness

There is a naked man
also walking
in complete darkness
like a river, shoving all
that moves or does not move
to the edge, the edge
itself to the edge, stones
trees, cliffs, fields, fence
lines, roads, cities, all shoved
to the edge and beyond
the edge, and once again
the naked man
reaches the end, alone
in darkness
like a waterfall, dark
moon, and even here
is unmoved as he moves.

Data

There is a naked man
sitting on his back porch
drinking a mug of tea
when all at once
he realizes
that everything
he has been thinking
and accepting as real
since the fiasco
in the delivery room
is just content

neutral content

like data
on a hard drive

which makes him wonder
what would happen
if he just hit delete
and dumped it all, like this:

The white bucks
covered with mud and all
childhood memories: Delete.

The car in the mud, cold
rain falling, the girl
with wet stringy
hair standing there and all
the other embarrassments
of a lifetime: Delete.

Mud itself: Delete.
Mother: Delete.
Father: Delete.
Guilt: Delete.

The Cold War: Delete.
Viet Nam: Delete.
The fifty-six Chevy: Downshift and Delete.
Arrests: Surrender and Delete.

The 1978 Yankees: Delete
    but first copy to another drive.

All the jobs
and the politics, the politics
of jobs, desire: Double Dog Delete.

Pointing dogs: Delete.

Food: Delete.
Beer: Delete.
Wine: Delete.
Whisky from the bright
heathery highlands: Delete
straight up in a snifter.

The mower: Delete.
The tiller: Delete.
The boat: Delete and Sunk.

Sex: Delete
    but tenderly.

Death: Delete.
Fear of death: Delete.

Fear of the fear of Death:
Delete, Delete, Delete

and on and on
through layer upon
layer, byte after
gigabyte, diving back down
the rabbit hole of his life
the naked man finally
arrives at the empty
disk, cold, hard, suddenly
silent, pristine, the gleaming
surface of absolute
zero, and then slowly
the disk itself
and the stars, one
by one by one
disappearing from empty
space, and then space itself
in a riot of pure Delete.

Breakfast

There is a naked man
staring through a blindfold
into the muzzles
of a dozen guns.

To this end, he has kept
his silence, and now
is ready to die.

His last cigarette, from years
ago, smolders on the ground
where he spit it out.

He joins his hands
to pray, where they are cuffed
behind his back.

A light breeze carries
the smell of someone's breakfast
cooking somewhere nearby

bacon, eggs, potatoes
and coffee, the scrape
of spatula, steel

on steel, the sweet
acidic scent
of the coffee.

Spectacle

There is a naked man
grieving the loss
prostrate on the sand.

Carrion birds
circle above him, again

worms dig from below.

Well behaved crowds
gather behind ropes
to watch, speaking
in muffled voices
about the naked man's
posture, the tears
that look like blood
swelling at the corners
of his eyes.

Tastefully, nearby
vendors sell funnel
cakes, popcorn, hot
dogs and beer, count
change and keep
their eyes on the weather.

Tight Spot

There is a naked man
wedged head down
in a shaft
of his own digging
deep inside the roots
of an ash tree
infected with borers
and dying
in the long afternoon
of a two-year drought.

The naked man's arms
are pinned at his sides, his head
is caught against a rock
he buried himself
years ago, and worms
and roots tickle
the ends of his hairs.

At this point
the naked man
has many regrets

not the least of which
was his decision
to cast aside the shovel
and begin digging
with his bare hands.

Way Beyond Armageddon

There is a naked man
riding the fast and mighty
Hippo of Pursuit out
of the ruined city
onto the steppes.

Ahead of them
a cloud of dust burns
deep vermillion
in the distance, ignited
by setting sun

and all night the naked
man and the hippo
press on as one
while the fire burns hot
then cold in the xeric
light of the rising moon

and on the third day, columns
of flame and smoke loom
as they charge straight through
without thinking
and disappear like drops
of water exploding
in hot oil, fragments
caught up in the wind
and scattered like seeds, way
beyond the moon, way
beyond the sun.

What No One Saw

Right before
the moment of truth
in the midst
of smoke and turmoil
there is a naked man
who leaps from the back
of the fast and mighty
Hippo of Pursuit
to the Ewe of Last Resort
and rides out
on a rising seam
from the valley
floor, climbing through flames
to where water
like shining stairs
rushes down
a canyon studded
with tiny blooms rooted
in ice: saxifrage
breaking way
for the Elegant
Polemonium, stinky
but eternal
Sky Pilot.

Etching

There is a naked man
walking uphill from the edge
of the stinking abyss.

All around him
the cataracts of doom
roar like dragons

flames explode against the sky
in great carnivorous
arcs, black clouds cover
the sun, rain falls down, stones
sizzle and melt.

The naked man's hair
is on fire, he is soaked
like a drowned rat
shit out by a shark
and his clothes hang from him
like rags dangling from nails

his face hangs like a fading
imprint of his face

and somehow
he has also lost one shoe
like someone famous once did
many years before.

Under the red sun

the last human being
on planet Earth blinks
and then walks out
from the pile of rocks
where he spent the night
just as the first one did
countless ages before.

It is the naked man himself.

He stretches and yawns, showing
his teeth to the sky.

At the edge of a stream
he leans down, blinks again
and remembers
his mother in the quick
turn of a fish
and the sudden way
the fish also
disappears.

About the Author

Robert Tremmel grew up in Northwest Iowa, studied at the University of Iowa, and is Emeritus Professor of English at Iowa State University. His most recent book of poems is *The Records of Kosho the Toad* from Bottom Dog Press, and he has published widely in both academic and literary journals and magazines. For the last twenty-three years, he and his wife, Michelle, have lived in Ankeny, Iowa, just a short drive from waters polluted by farm run-off from Northwest Iowa.

Notes and Acknowledgments

"Way Beyond Armageddon" was first published in *Lalitamba* and later collected in *There is a Naked Man*, published by Main Street Rag.

"Early 21st Century" was first published in *Rattle*.

"majorpsychosisthreshold" is borrowed from "Seven AM Blue Funk: A Hangover Poem" by John Birkbeck. Birkbeck was an Iowa City poet and a leading figure in late-night limerick competitions held many years ago at Harold Donnelly's fine drinking establishment.

"Spectacle" and "Saturday Night" were first published in *Santa Fe Literary Review*.

"The Good Old Days" was First Published in *Packingtown Review*.

"Data" was first published in *Wisconsin Review*.

"Alternate Ending" was first published in *Hotel Amerika*.

"Tuning Into the Past" and "Near Death Experience" were first published in *Sport Literate*.

"Walking in Complete Darkness" is based on a passage from Shohaku Okumura's *Living by Vow*.

> "But there was one stretch
> of several hundred meters
> covered by evergreens
> that was completely dark."

Note also Hunter S. Thompson's insight: "There is no honest way to explain it because the only people who really know where it is are the ones who have gone over."

"Toad in the Snow" is based on a line from Kusan Sunim: "The toad in the snow catches and swallows the tiger."

Our Mission

BRICK ROAD

POETRY PRESS

The mission of Brick Road Poetry Press is to publish and promote poetry that entertains, amuses, edifies, and surprises a wide audience of appreciative readers. We are not qualified to judge who deserves to be published, so we concentrate on publishing what we enjoy. Our preference is for poetry geared toward dramatizing the human experience in language rich with sensory image and metaphor, recognizing that poetry can be, at one and the same time, both familiar as the perspiration of daily labor and as outrageous as a carnival sideshow.

Available from Brick Road Poetry Press

BRICK ROAD
POETRY PRESS

www.brickroadpoetrypress.com

The Word in Edgewise by Sean M. Conrey

Household Inventory by Connie Jordan Green

Practice by Richard M. Berlin

A Meal Like That by Albert Garcia

Cracker Sonnets by Amy Wright

Things Seen by Joseph Stanton

Battle Sleep by Shannon Tate Jonas

Lauren Bacall Shares a Limousine by Susan J. Erickson

Ambushing Water by Danielle Hanson

Having and Keeping by David Watts

Assisted Living by Erin Murphy

Credo by Steve McDonald

The Deer's Bandanna by David Oates

Creation Story by Steven Owen Shields

Touring the Shadow Factory by Gary Stein

American Mythology by Raphael Kosek

Waxing the Dents by Daniel Edward Moore

Speaking Parts by Beth Ruscio

Escape Envy by Ace Boggess

Also Available from Brick Road Poetry Press

BRICK ROAD

POETRY PRESS

www.brickroadpoetrypress.com

Dancing on the Rim by Clela Reed

Possible Crocodiles by Barry Marks

Pain Diary by Joseph D. Reich

Otherness by M. Ayodele Heath

Drunken Robins by David Oates

Damnatio Memoriae by Michael Meyerhofer

Lotus Buffet by Rupert Fike

The Melancholy MBA by Richard Donnelly

Two-Star General by Grey Held

Chosen by Toni Thomas

Etch and Blur by Jamie Thomas

Water-Rites by Ann E. Michael

Bad Behavior by Michael Steffen

Tracing the Lines by Susanna Lang

Rising to the Rim by Carol Tyx

Treading Water with God by Veronica Badowski

Rich Man's Son by Ron Self

Just Drive by Robert Cooperman

The Alp at the End of My Street by Gary Leising

About the Prize

The Brick Road Poetry Prize, established in 2010, is awarded annually for the best book-length poetry manuscript. Entries are accepted August 1st through November 1st. The winner receives $1000 and publication. For details on our preferences and the complete submission guidelines, please visit our website at www.brickroadpoetrypress.com.

Winners of the Brick Road Poetry Prize

2019

Return of the Naked Man by Robert Tremmel

2018

Speaking Parts by Beth Ruscio

2017

Touring the Shadow Factory by Gary Stein

2016

Assisted Living by Erin Murphy

2015

Lauren Bacall Shares a Limousine by Susan J. Erickson

2014

Battle Sleep by Shannon Tate Jonas

2013

Household Inventory by Connie Jordan Green

2012

The Alp at the End of My Street by Gary Leising

2011

Bad Behavior by Michael Steffen

2010

Damnatio Memoriae by Michael Meyerhofer